I See God!
Through Children's Eyes

Patricia Johnson

I SEE GOD! Through Children's Eyes

Copyright © 2025 by Patricia Johnson

Illustrated by Salma Designs.

Edits and design by Dominion Unlimited Editorial Services.

Inspired by: Holy Spirit Instruction.

Scripture quotations taken from The Holy Bible, New International Reader's Version®, NIrV® Copyright © 1995, 1996, 1998, 2014 by Biblica, Inc. used with permission of Zondervan. www.zondervan.com

Published by Dominion Unlimited Publications.

Dedicated To

The children of The World, my inspiring husband Frederick Johnson, my son Erience Dickerson, my apostle Dr. Bj Baker, my pastor Lonzine Lee, and my late apostle Shirley Manigault-Turpin.

To GOD Be The Glory.

A Note from Patricia Johnson

This book was inspired by Holy Spirit Instruction:
The years I spent in child care have been both a unique experience and a blessing in my life. Children are special people. They see things in a different light. How they interact and hear and often see things, and how they express love.

Contents

Hills, Streams, and Daffodils	9
Snails and Mountain Trails	13
Sunshine and Rain	16
The Sky, Birds, And Mom's Apple Pie	19
Oceans and Emotions	23
Mothers and Fathers	26
You And Me	28
The Moon, Stars, And Your Twinkling Eyes	30
Trees And Bumble Bees	33
God's Word	36
All The Things We Do	37
About the Author	40

Hills, Streams, and Daffodils

I see GOD in the hills,

I see God! Hills, Streams, and Daffodils

and in the streams

and in the yellow daffodils.

Do you see Him too?

I see God!   Hills, Streams, and Daffodils

> Remember the wonderful things he has done. Remember his miracles and how he judged our enemies
>
> 1 Chronicles 16:12

Snails and Mountain Trails

I see GOD in the snails,

I see God!

Snails and Mountain Trails

and in the mountain trails.

Do you see Him too?

The blessing of the LORD brings wealth. Trouble doesn't come with it

Proverbs 10:22

Sunshine and Rain

I see GOD in the sunshine,

and in the rain.

His love is shining through in all that we do.

Do you see Him too?

I see God!   Snails and Mountain Trails

> The true light that gives light to every man was coming into the world.
>
> John 1:9

The Sky, Birds, And Mom's Apple Pie

I see GOD in the sky,

I see God!   The Sky, Birds, And Mom's Apple Pie

and in the birds that fly

I see God! The Sky, Birds, And Mom's Apple Pie

and my Mom's apple pie!

Do you see Him too?

I see God!   The Sky, Birds, And Mom's Apple Pie

Give us today our daily bread

Matthew 6:11

Oceans and Emotions

I see GOD in the ocean,

I see God!   Oceans and Emotions

and in my emotions.

Do you see Him too?

I see God!   Oceans and Emotions

> Trust in the LORD and do good. Then you will live in the land and enjoy its food.
> Find your delight in the LORD. Then he will give you everything your heart really wants.
>
> Psalm 37:3 and 4

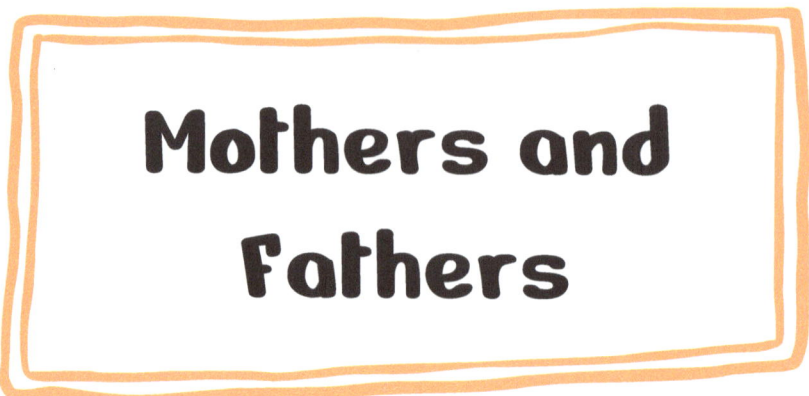

I see GOD in my mother and my father too! Thank You. I will honor them.

Do you see them too?

I see God!   Mothers and Fathers

As for every man to receive his heritage and rejoice in his labor - This is the gift of GOD.

Ecclesiastes 3:22

You and me

I see GOD in you and in me.

His love will sing a song of joy for you and for me.

Do you see Him too?

I see God!   **You and me**

> Lord, I have always trusted in your kindness, I will yet celebrate with passion and joy when your salvation lifts me up. I will sing my song of joy to you, the Most High, for in all of this you have strengthened my soul. My enemies say that I have no Savior, but I know that I have one in you!
>
> Psalm 13: 5 and 6

The Moon, Stars, And Your Twinkling Eyes

I see GOD in the moon,

I see God!   The Moon, Stars, And Your Twinkling Eyes

the stars,

and in the *twinkling of your eyes*!

Do you see Him too?

I see God!   The Moon, Stars, And Your Twinkling Eyes

> I have come into this world that those who do not see may see.
>
> John 9:39

Trees And Bumble Bees

I see GOD in the trees,

and in the bumble bees!

Do you see Him too?

I see God!   Trees And Bumble Bees

> Your status stands firm, holiness adorns your house, for endless days.
>
> Psalm 93:5

God's Word

I heard GOD's Word and how
He tells you of the good news.

Do you hear Him too?

All The Things We Do

We see GOD in all the things that we do.

And He sees us too!

Behold, what manner of love The Father has bestowed on us, that we should be called children of GOD!

1 John 3:1

Amen!

About the Author

 Patricia Johnson is a caring and gifted storyteller with over 20 years of experience nurturing young hearts as the owner of a licensed Group Family Day Care. Her humility, compassion, and deep love for God shine through in everything she does.

Patricia has served as a liaison between the Administration for Children's Services (A.C.S.) and child care providers across New York City—supporting informal, family, and group family day care programs.

Her dedication to children and families has touched countless lives. One thing Patricia truly loves is sharing and seeing God through the eyes of children. A loving wife, mother, and grandmother, she enjoys life, love, and ministry with her husband Frederick. They reside in Brooklyn, New York.

www.ingramcontent.com/pod-product-compliance
Lightning Source LLC
Chambersburg PA
CBHW061400090426
42743CB00002B/84